DEEP SEA EXPLORATION

Richard Spilsbury

Published 2010 by
A & C Black Publishers Ltd.
36 Soho Square, London, W1D 3QY

www.acblack.com

ISBN   HB 978-1-4081-2432-1
       PB 978-1-4081-2691-2

Series consultant: Gill Matthews

This book is produced using paper that is made from wood grown in managed, sustainable forests. It is natural, renewable and recyclable. The logging and manufacturing processes conform to the environmental regulations of the country of origin.

Produced for A & C Black by Calcium. www.calciumcreative.co.uk

Printed and bound in China by C&C Offset Printing Co.

All the internet addresses given in this book were correct at the time of going to press. The author and publishers regret any inconvenience caused if addresses have changed or sites have ceased to exist, but can accept no responsibility for any such changes.

Acknowledgements

The publishers would like to thank the following for their kind permission to reproduce their photographs:

Cover: Corbis: Jeffrey Rotman. **Pages:** Corbis: Jeffrey Rotman 7, Denis Scott 18, Paul Souders 9t; FLPA: Luciano Candisani/Minden Pictures 17; Fotolia: Kurt De Bruyn 28, Richard Carey 10, 13t, Juergen Rudorf 9b, Ilan Ben Tov 21; Istockphoto: Geoffrey Hollman 4–32, Jodi Jacobson 8; NOAA: 13b, 22b, 27, Ian MacDonald, Texas A & M University, Corpus Christi 24, National Undersea Research Program (NURP) 29t, OAR/NURP 25, OAR/NURP/University of Connecticut 26, OAR/NURP/Woods Hole Oceanographic Institute 29b; Photoshot: NHPA 5; Rex Features: 20; Shutterstock: Anton Bryksin 19t, A Cotton Photo 4, Grivina 4–32, Lijuan Guo 16t, Ivanova Inga 19b, Bill Kennedy 16b, Mana Photo 22t, Niar 15t, Sergey Popov V 14, Roman & Olexandra 12, Ian Scott 11t, Elisei Shafer 15b, Morozova Tatyana (Manamana) 6, 11b.

Illustrations: Geoff Ward.

CONTENTS

SECRETS OF THE DEEP

Deep beneath the blue surface of the oceans lies an inky-black world. Some of the most fascinating creatures on Earth have been found in these dark, icy waters. Many more may swim there, as yet undiscovered. Our mission is to journey to these depths to find them – are you ready for the trip of a lifetime?

Bottlenose dolphins swim in groups near the ocean surface.

 # What did we find?

Underwater mountains

Scientists have found out that the ocean floor is smooth and flat in some areas, but covered in underwater mountains in others. Some of these mountains are thousands of metres high but do not even stick out of the water!

Weird and wonderful creatures such as this hatchet fish live in the deep waters of the world's oceans.

THE RIGHT EQUIPMENT

If we had tried to dive to the ocean's depth in our wetsuits, the **pressure** would have crushed our lungs! Instead, we travelled in a **submersible** – a diving machine designed for the deep sea.

Look out for our submersible – it will show how deep we are.

Sunlight zone	0–200m, plenty of light
Twilight zone	200–1000m, a little light
Midnight zone	1000–4000m, hardly any light
Dark zone	4000–5000+m, no light

trench

OUR SCUBA KIT

- Wetsuit protects diver from cold water, but not from deep sea pressure.
- Air tank provides oxygen for a few hours, but not long enough to travel to deep sea.
- Flippers to help diver swim further, but not for hundreds of metres.

The deeper underwater you go, the greater pressure there is. **SCUBA** divers can only dive safely to about 50 metres.

Our submersible

- Thick steel walls to withstand the high pressures of the deep sea.
- Tough but thin crystal window instead of thick glass.
- Big compressed air tanks: 30 litres (6½ gallons) per person per minute, plus more in case of emergency.
- Propellers to move us in different directions underwater.
- Lights and cameras
- Grab arms to pick up deep sea samples.

A submersible looks a little like an armoured spacecraft!

FEEDING FRENZY

We sank beneath the ocean's surface in our submersible. Straight away we saw a turtle slowly swimming by and then a large, shimmering shoal of small fish.

Predators and prey

The fish had been eating **plankton**, which are tiny floating plants and animals. They were now being attacked. Seabirds dived into the water to peck at the fish. Large tuna fish, dolphins, sealions, and even a humpback whale swam into the shoal to catch their **prey**. This was an ocean feeding frenzy!

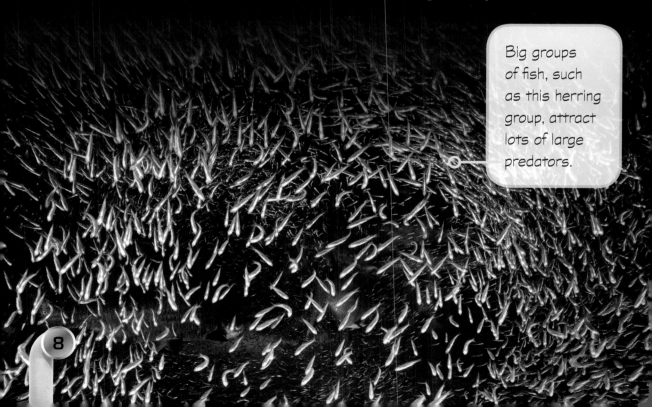

Big groups of fish, such as this herring group, attract lots of large predators.

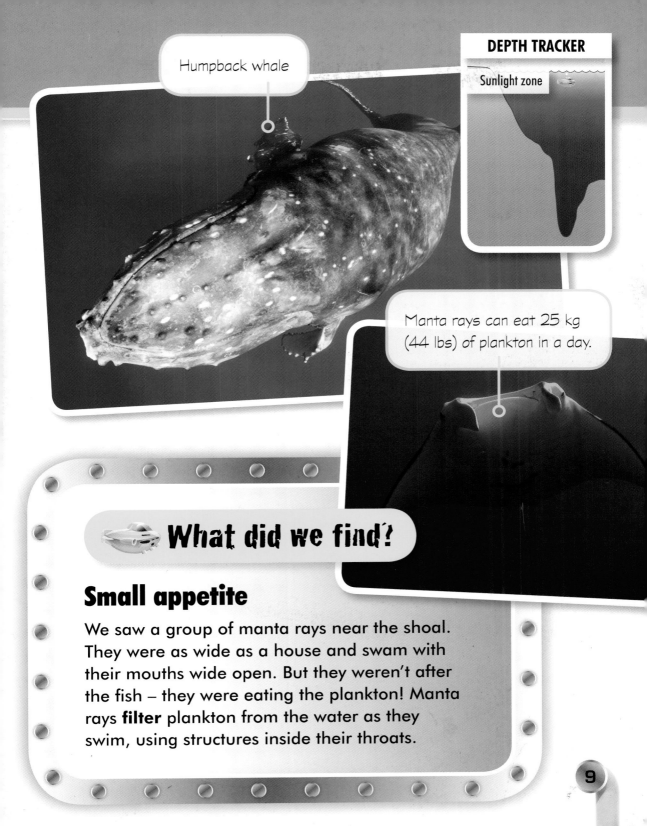

Humpback whale

Manta rays can eat 25 kg (44 lbs) of plankton in a day.

What did we find?

Small appetite

We saw a group of manta rays near the shoal. They were as wide as a house and swam with their mouths wide open. But they weren't after the fish – they were eating the plankton! Manta rays **filter** plankton from the water as they swim, using structures inside their throats.

REEF LIFE

An hour later a reef shark surprised us while we were swimming outside the submerisble to look at a **coral reef** in shallow water. The shark swam close enough for us to look into its black eyes and check out its sharp teeth.

Underwater community

The reef is home to an underwater community. We saw starfish feeding on the coral and colourful fish nibbling on seaweeds. One section of reef appeared to move and I then realized it was not part of the reef, but an octopus instead!

An octopus can change its skin colour to match the area that it is hiding on.

Reef shark

Corals grow in many different shapes and colours.

What did we find?

Coral reef

Reefs can look like strange rocky plants, but they are made by animals called coral polyps. They build hard coral shelters around their bodies in light, warm seawater. The coral builds up over many years to create reefs. Reefs look tough but they are fragile and easily damaged. We were very careful as we swam back to the submersible.

SHIPWRECK!

As we dropped towards the seafloor we saw the wreck of a ship. At the front there was a jagged hole. We guessed that the ship may have sunk because it hit the reef.

Scallop

 What did we find?

Seafloor life

A spider crab was crawling along the seafloor near the shipwreck, balancing on its long legs. The mud of the seafloor is full of life, which is tasty food for some creatures. Sure enough, the spider crab found some scallops. They looked like swimming false teeth as they tried to escape!

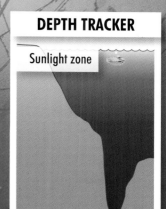

There are about 3 million shipwrecks in oceans around the world.

Frozen in time

We peered inside the ship through the windows – it was like it had been frozen in time. One cabin had a picture on the wall, half covered by a starfish. In another room we saw broken crockery, tins of food, and a stove, all with yellow **sponges** clinging to them.

The *Titanic* is one of the most famous of all shipwrecks.

EEL ENCOUNTER

As we swam past the hole in the shipwreck, a pointed face poked out, with its mouth wide open. It was an eel. We watched as its long, spotted body turned and swam back into the gloom of the ship.

Safe inside

Shoals of big, bullet-shaped barracuda fish were hunting for food outside the wreck. We saw that other fish stayed inside. Shipwrecks are a bit like artificial reefs. There are lots of hiding places for animals to keep out of the way of **predators**. Seahorses slowly moved amongst the corals, sponges and weeds that grew on the ship.

Barracudas are fast-swimming fish with razor-sharp teeth.

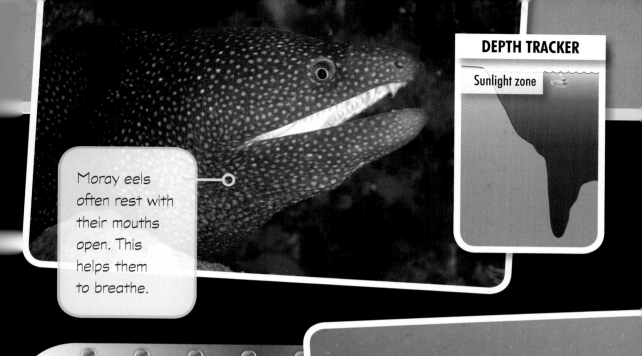

Moray eels often rest with their mouths open. This helps them to breathe.

Sunlight zone

 ## What did we find?

Poisonous lion

The lion fish is only about 30 cm (12 in) long but it came right up to the submersible. It is a beautiful striped fish with lots of long, pointed spines. It was unafraid because its spines are weapons. If one jabbed you it would really hurt and make you very ill.

TWILIGHT ZONE

We pressed our faces to the glass of a side window and looked into the dark. We could see the flashing lights of cuttlefish and jellyfish. The rounded top of one jellyfish must have been 2 metres (about 6 ft) across. Thank goodness we were inside the submersible and out of reach of all those stinging tentacles.

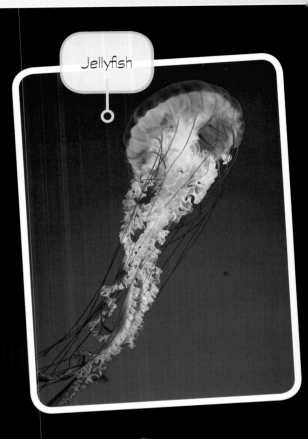

Jellyfish

Cuttlefish send messages to each other by flashing light in the dark.

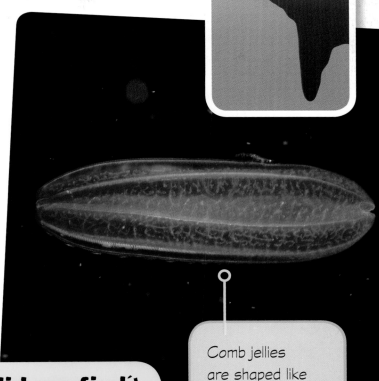

Deeper and darker

We had reached the twilight zone of the ocean about half a kilometre (¼ mile) down. Only a tiny amount of sunlight can reach these depths. Outside the temperature was dropping and the pressure was rising as we went deeper.

Comb jellies are shaped like gooseberries and glow in the dark.

 What did we find?

Lighting up the deep

Many deep sea animals produce their own light. Chemicals in their bodies mix and react to release light, rather like glow sticks. The animals make light for different reasons. Some use light to find their way in the dark, others to attract mates or to draw prey closer so they can eat them.

BATTLE OF THE GIANTS

At 800 metres (2,600 ft) deep there was a huge whack on the side of the submersible. We rushed to look through the window and saw a giant squid! Its **tentacles** were trying to grip on to the submersible. This animal must have been 10 metres (32 ft) long.

Squid hunter!

Just then, an even bigger shape appeared fast out of the darkness. It was a sperm whale and it was hunting the squid. The squid tried to get away but the whale grabbed it firmly.

Sperm whales can stay underwater for more than two hours.

What did we find?

Swimming deep

Whales need to breathe air to survive. A whale takes many huge gulps of air before it dives. It stores most of the oxygen from the air in its muscles and blood.

SQUID EYES

A giant squid's eyes can be as big as a soccer ball! They are like headlights to help the squid see in the dark.

19

We eventually reached deep, black water. We came across an angler fish. The tip of the antennae above its mouth looked like a wiggling piece of tasty food. The angler fish was also lit up. It was ready to snap up any fish attracted by this clever trick.

Adapted for eating

There is not much food for animals down here, so predators need special features to help them survive in the dark. The angler fish has its light. The deep sea gulper has wide jaws. It can fit a much larger animal than itself in its mouth.

Most angler fish are only the size of a person's fist.

Midnight zone

Sea cucumbers chew up any bits of dead animals that fall to the ocean floor.

What did we find?

Deep sea suckers

We saw strange marks, a bit like tyre tracks, across the ocean floor. We realized that sea cucumbers were leaving tracks as they slowly moved along. Sea cucumbers suck up mud on the ocean floor into their stomachs, to extract any hidden bits of food that might be in the mud.

SHOCK IN THE OCEAN

Without any warning the submersible suddenly lurched to the side, and was out of control. It tumbled against a rock and the lights went off for a moment. It must have been an underwater earthquake.

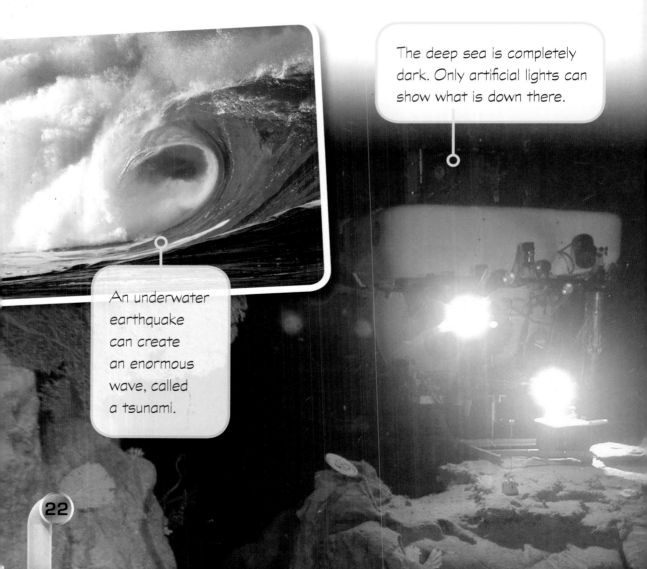

The deep sea is completely dark. Only artificial lights can show what is down there.

An underwater earthquake can create an enormous wave, called a tsunami.

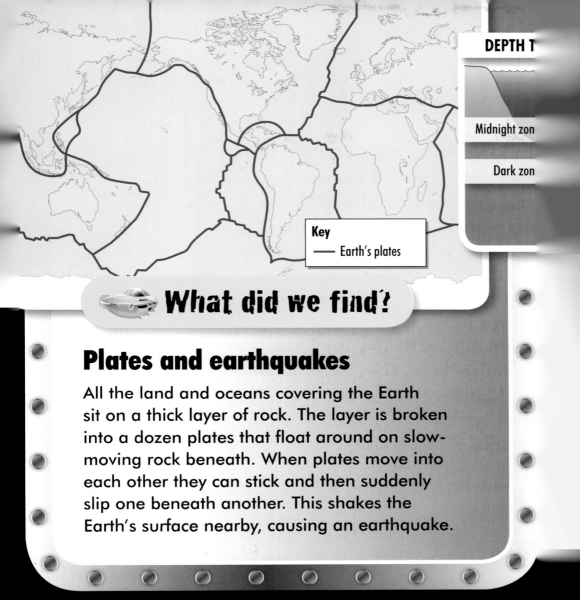

Key
— Earth's plates

What did we find?

Plates and earthquakes

All the land and oceans covering the Earth sit on a thick layer of rock. The layer is broken into a dozen plates that float around on slow-moving rock beneath. When plates move into each other they can stick and then suddenly slip one beneath another. This shakes the Earth's surface nearby, causing an earthquake.

Growing rock

We just saw some rock growing! We were at a place where plates were pulling apart. This left a crack through which liquid rock was seeping from inside the Earth. It soon cooled down in the cold seawater and set hard. So this is how underwater mountains can grow

Out of the window we saw pale **crabs**, **mussels**, and long red **tubeworms** clustered around what looked like a chimney with black smoke coming out of it. This was a **hydrothermal vent**.

Extreme food web

The vent was hot and full of bits of dissolved rocks called **minerals**. Tiny living things called **bacteria** thrive there. They make food from the minerals. Mussels filter the bacteria from the water, then eat them. Crabs and other creatures feed on the mussels.

Red tubeworms live near hydrothermal vents. They can grow to be taller than a man!

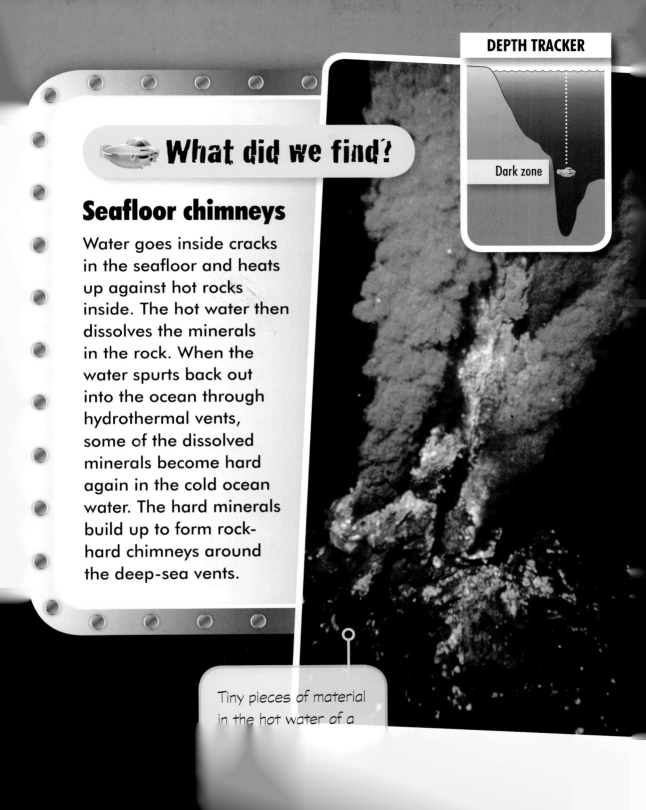

What did we find?

Seafloor chimneys

Water goes inside cracks in the seafloor and heats up against hot rocks inside. The hot water then dissolves the minerals in the rock. When the water spurts back out into the ocean through hydrothermal vents, some of the dissolved minerals become hard again in the cold ocean water. The hard minerals build up to form rock-hard chimneys around the deep-sea vents.

Tiny pieces of material in the hot water of a

OVER THE EDGE

Suddenly the seafloor in front of us just disappeared. We had reached the edge of an ocean trench. Trenches are dips in the seafloor caused by one plate moving underneath another one. They are the deepest places on Earth.

Reaching the limit

We dropped over the edge and fell fast. Soon we were 7,000 metres (23,000 ft) deep. The water pressure here was 700 times greater than at the ocean surface. The lights shone on some giant isopods – crab-like creatures that live in deep water.

This submarine has reached the bottom of a deep sea trench.

NURP 1

Deepest trench known

The trench we explored was small compared to the Mariana trench, near Japan. The bottom of the Mariana is around 11,000 metres (36,100 ft) deep. The pressure on a submersible in a trench this deep is the same as having 48 jumbo jets stacked on it. Only one submersible with passengers has ever been taken there, and that had steel walls 13 cm (5 inches) thick.

Dark zone

Giant isopod

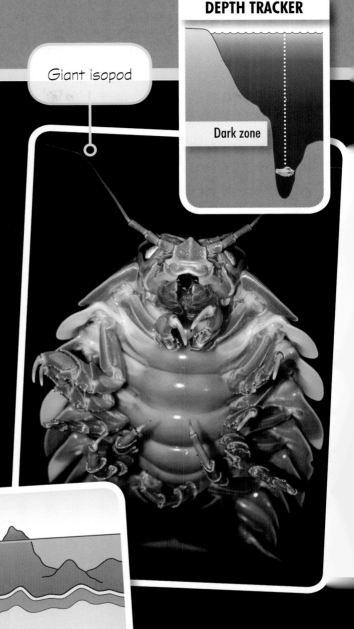

The Mariana trench was formed when two plates pushed together to create a deep cut in the seabed.

DEEP SEA DISCOVERY

Last night we finally returned to the surface. We took with us some of the bacteria we found in the sea vents. This may help scientists to find out more about other, harmful bacterias.

Ocean around us

As we surfaced we saw fishing boats pulling along a giant net. People are catching so many fish that there are not many left of some species. Trawler nets can damage reefs and harm sea life. Scientists and fishing crews must work together to care for the oceans.

Huge amounts of fish and other sea creatures are caught in fishing boat nets.

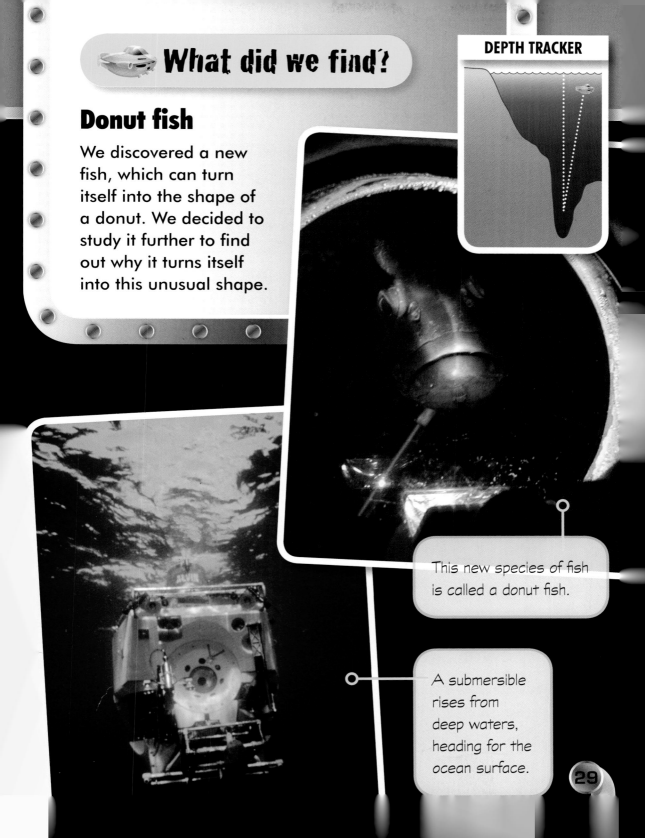

What did we find?

Donut fish

We discovered a new fish, which can turn itself into the shape of a donut. We decided to study it further to find out why it turns itself into this unusual shape.

DEPTH TRACKER

This new species of fish is called a donut fish.

A submersible rises from deep waters, heading for the ocean surface.

GLOSSARY

bacteria very simple microscopic living things

coral reef underwater feature mainly found in warm seas, made of the skeletons of coral animals

crab type of ten-legged animal with a tough shell, claws, and eyes on short stalks, usually found on shores or the seafloor

filter to pass liquid through a fine barrier so that it is let through, but solid pieces are trapped in the barrier

hydrothermal vent an opening in Earth's crust, deep beneath the ocean surface

mineral natural substance that makes up rocks

mussel type of animal with two hinged, long shells, mostly found on the seafloor and rocks

plankton mixture of tiny plants and animals that drift or float through the oceans

predator animal that hunts and eats other animals, such as a shark

pressure force pressing against something, such as the force of water on someone diving

prey animal that is eaten by other animals, such as a herring

SCUBA short for 'self contained underwater breathing apparatus'

sponge marine animals that live together in a blob-like shape with holes over the surface through which they take in food

submersible vessel that can dive, often taking people, deep underwater

tentacle long organ near the mouth of animals including octopus and anemones, which they use to feel, feed, or grasp

tubeworm type of marine worm that lives in a hard tube it makes

FURTHER INFORMATION

Websites
Find out more about deep sea life at:
www.teachers.ash.org.au/jmresources/deep/creatures.html or
http://deepsealife.net/

People have used all sorts of submersibles to explore the oceans.
To learn more, visit:
www.pbs.org/wgbh/nova/abyss/frontier/deepsea.html

Would you like to know more about the world's oceans, the life
they hold, and the problems they face? One place to start is:
www.panda.org/about_our_earth/blue_planet/

Books
Monsters of the Deep: Deep Sea Adaptation by Kelly Regan
Barnhill. Fact Finders (2008).

Extreme Science: Life in the Crusher by Trevor Day.
A & C Black (2009).

Underwater Exploration (Restless Sea) by Carole Garbuny Vogel.
Children's Press (2003).

DVD
Blue Planet, narrated by David Attenborough (BBC, 2005)

INDEX

Louis Braille

Jayne Woodhouse

First published in Great Britain by Heinemann Library
Halley Court, Jordan Hill, Oxford OX2 8EJ,
a division of Reed Educational and Professional Publishing Ltd.

OXFORD FLORENCE PRAGUE MADRID ATHENS
MELBOURNE AUCKLAND KUALA LUMPUR SINGAPORE TOKYO
IBADAN NAIROBI KAMPALA JOHANNESBURG GABORONE
PORTSMOUTH NH (USA) CHICAGO MEXICO CITY SAO PAULO

Designed by Ken Vail Graphic Design, Cambridge.
Illustrations by Hemesh Alles
Printed and bound in Malaysia by Times Offset (M) Sdn. Bhd.

01 00 99 98 97
10 9 8 7 6 5 4 3 2 1

ISBN 0 431 02472 3

Some words are shown in bold, **like this**.
You can find out what they mean by looking
in the glossary. The glossary also helps you
say difficult words.

British Library Cataloguing in Publication Data

Woodhouse, Jayne
Louis Braille. - (Lives & times)
1. Braille, Louis, 1805–1852 - Juvenile literature
2. Educators - France - Biography - Juvenile literature
3. Braille - History - Juvenile literature
I. Title
362.4'1'092

Acknowledgements
The Publishers would like to thank the following for permission to reproduce photographs:
Eye Ubiquitous/Paul Seheult, pp.17, 18, 19, 20, 21, 22, 23

Cover photograph: Mary Evans Picture Library

Our thanks to Betty Root for her comments in the preparation of this book.

Every effort has been made to contact copyright holders of any material reproduced in this book.
Any omissions will be rectified in subsequent printings if notice is given to the Publisher.

Contents

The first part of this book tells you the story of Louis Braille.
The second part tells you how we can find out about his life.

What is braille?

Do you know how blind people read?
They use books written in **braille**. The
books have little raised dots instead of
letters. The children read with their
fingers, not their eyes.

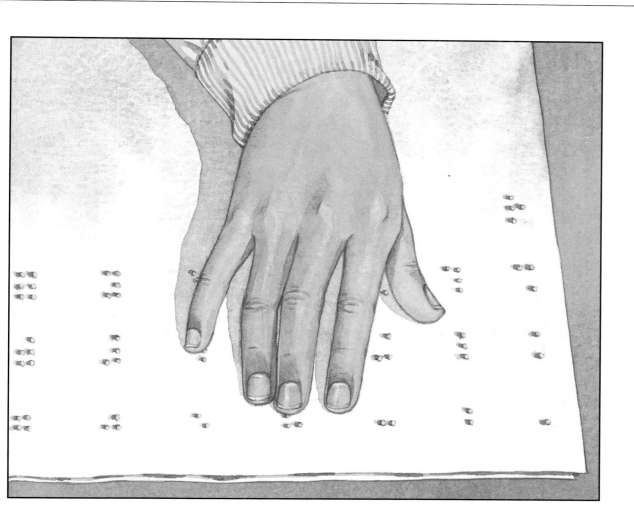

Braille is named after **Louis Braille**, the man who invented this special writing for blind people. This is his story.

Childhood

Louis Braille was born in France in 1809, nearly 200 years ago. His father was a **saddler**.

When he was a little boy, Louis loved to play in his father's workshop. 'Don't touch the knives!' said his father. 'They are too sharp for you.'

A terrible accident

One day, when he was three, Louis picked up a knife. He tried to cut with it. But the knife slipped and went into his eye.

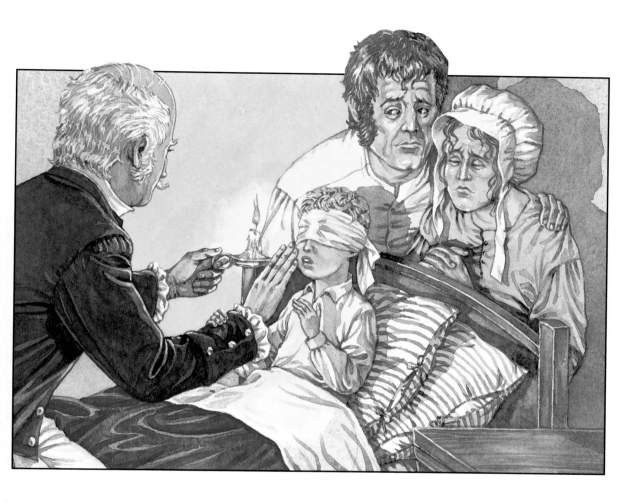

Then his other eye began to hurt too. The
doctor could not help. Soon Louis could
not see. He was blind.

Going to school

When Louis was ten, he went to a special school for blind children. It was in **Paris**, a long way away from his home.

Louis learnt to read with great big books.
The letters stood out. He had to feel each
letter with his fingers. It was very slow and
very hard.

A wonderful idea

Louis wanted to find a quicker way to read.

When he was only 13, he had a clever idea.

'I will change the letters into dots,' he said.

'Then they will be easier to feel.'

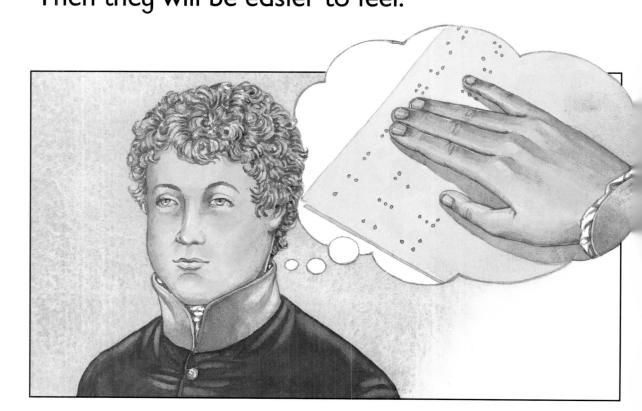

Louis made up a pattern of dots for each letter. He made a special ruler to press the dots into the paper. The dots stuck out so you could feel them. Now reading and writing were much easier.

Developing braille

But the teachers did not like Louis's idea.
'You cannot use this here!' they said.

When Louis grew up, he became a teacher
at the school. He never forgot his idea. He
made it better and better.

Louis dies

Louis was very sad that no-one liked his idea for making reading and writing easier. He was ill for a long time. He died when he was only 43.

A	B	C	D	E	F	G	H	I	J
K	L	M	N	O	P	Q	R	S	T
U	V	X	Y	Z	and	for	of	the	with

W	Oblique stroke	Numeral sign	Poetry sign		Apostrophe sign		Hyphen		
	;	:	.	,	!	( )	? "	"	

Not long after his death, people saw that Louis's dots really were a good idea. Today blind people all over the world use **braille** to read and write.

Portraits and artefacts

This is a **portrait** of Louis Braille.

It shows you what he looked like.

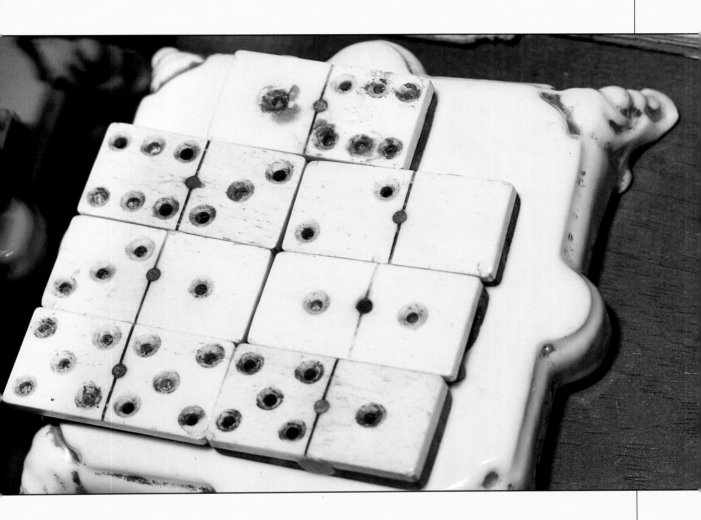

These are some dominoes that Louis
played with. You can see them in the
house where Louis was born.

Museums and artefacts

You can still see the house where Louis was born. It is now a **museum**. Inside, you can see some of his family's belongings, like his dominoes.

This is the workshop where Louis's father
worked. Look at all the sharp tools.
It was here, with one of these tools, that
Louis hurt his eye.

Buildings

The special school for the blind which Louis went to is still there in **Paris**. Here is a photograph of it today.

If you ever go to Paris, you can visit the **tomb** where Louis Braille is buried. It is in a famous building called the **Panthéon.** The tomb tells you when he died.

Glossary

This glossary explains difficult words, and tells you how to say words which are hard to say.

artefacts things which people make and use, like tools, clothes and cooking pots. We can learn about the past by looking at old artefacts. You say *arty-facts*

braille raised dots on paper which blind people use to read and write. You say *breyl*

Louis Braille you say *loo-ee breyl* (French people say *bry*)

museum building that has lots of **artefacts** in it which tell us about the past

Panthéon a building in Paris where you can see the tombs of many famous people. You say *pan-they-on*

Paris the capital city of France

portrait picture of a person, showing their face

saddler a person who makes and repairs saddles and leather harnesses for horses

tomb where a dead person is buried

Index